# Beach Toy

Find the toy.

# It's in the Bag

Put the bear in the bag.

# Halloween Friends

Help the friend find his buddy.

# Flying Home

Show the bird to its home.

# Scarecrows

Help the scarecrow find her friend.

# The Chick

Help the chick through the egg.

# The Henhouse

Find a path to the henhouse.

# The Tree

Lead the family to the tree.

# Butterflies

Color a path to the flowers.

# Owl Friends

Help the owl find his friends.

# Time to Eat

Color a path from the bread to the boy.

# Tea Time

Fill the cups with tea.

# Top to Bottom

Help the monkey out of the jungle gym.

# Popcorn Party

Color a path to the bowl of popcorn.

# Sweets

Color a path to the sweets.

# Hurry Home

Help the duck find her way home.

# Camping

Color a path to the camp.

# Hide and Seek

Help the pig find her friends.

# Missing Treats

Find the candy.

# Let's Sing

Color a path to the music.

# Pyramids

Lead the camel to the pyramids.

# Lion Tamer

Color a path to the lion.

# Hot Soup

Color a path to the pot of soup.

# Rainbow Road

Color the road to the rainbow.

# On the Farm

Help the cow to the hay.

# Lizard Fun

Help the lizard to the stump.

# School Days

Find a way to the school.

# Sip! Sip!

Help the mouse to the milk shake.

# Breakfast Time

Color a path to the bowl.

# Fun at the Park

Color the path to the bottom of the ride.

# Jump! Jump!

Help the mouse to the jump rope.

# Time to Land

Land the balloon.

# Dinosaur Friends

Help the dinosaur find his friend.

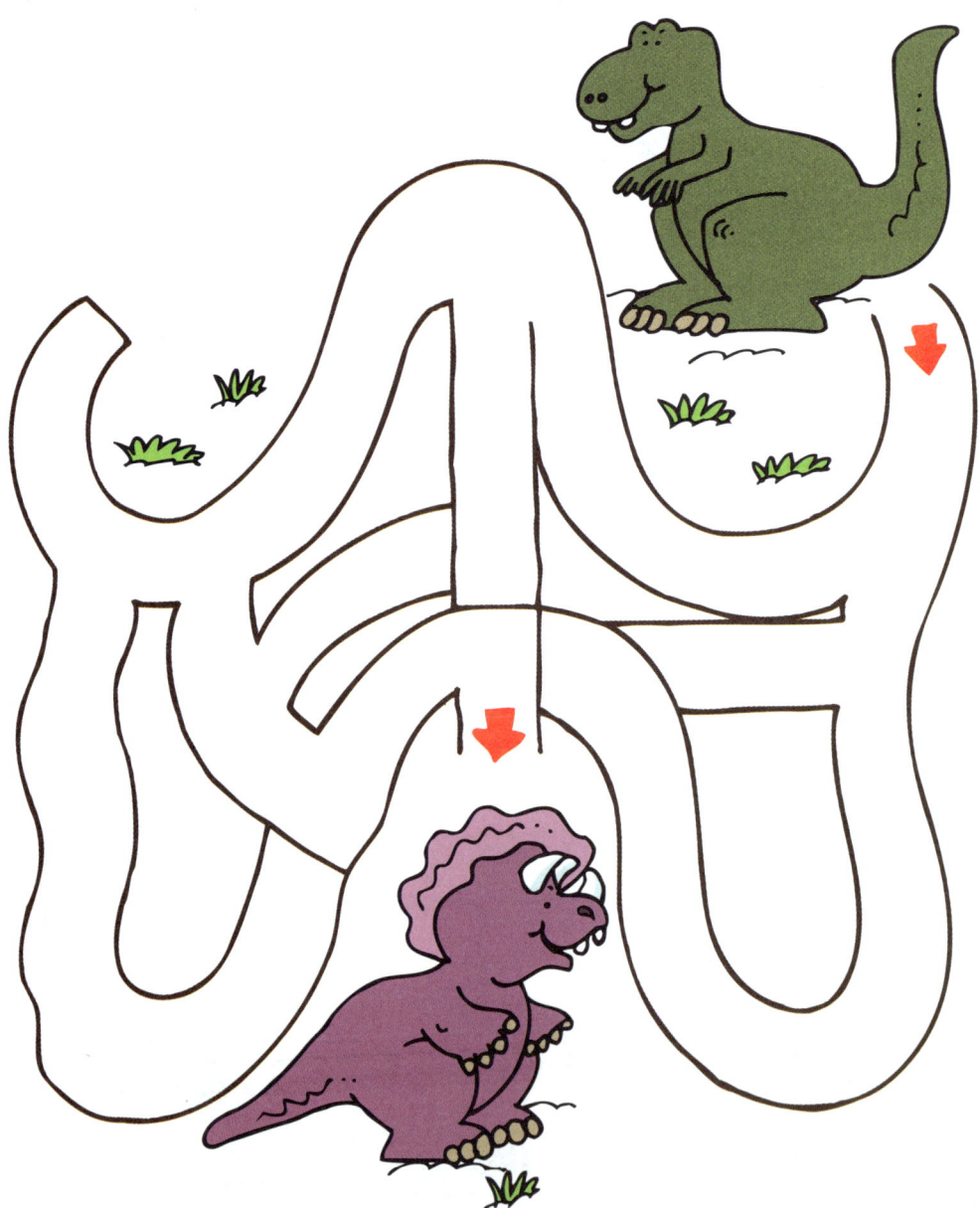

# Ice Cream

Color a path to the ice cream.

# Ho! Ho! Ho!

Lead Santa to his reindeer.

# Tractor Trip

Take the tractor to the barn.

# Pin the Tail

Color a path to the lion.

# A Hole in One

Hit the ball into the hole.

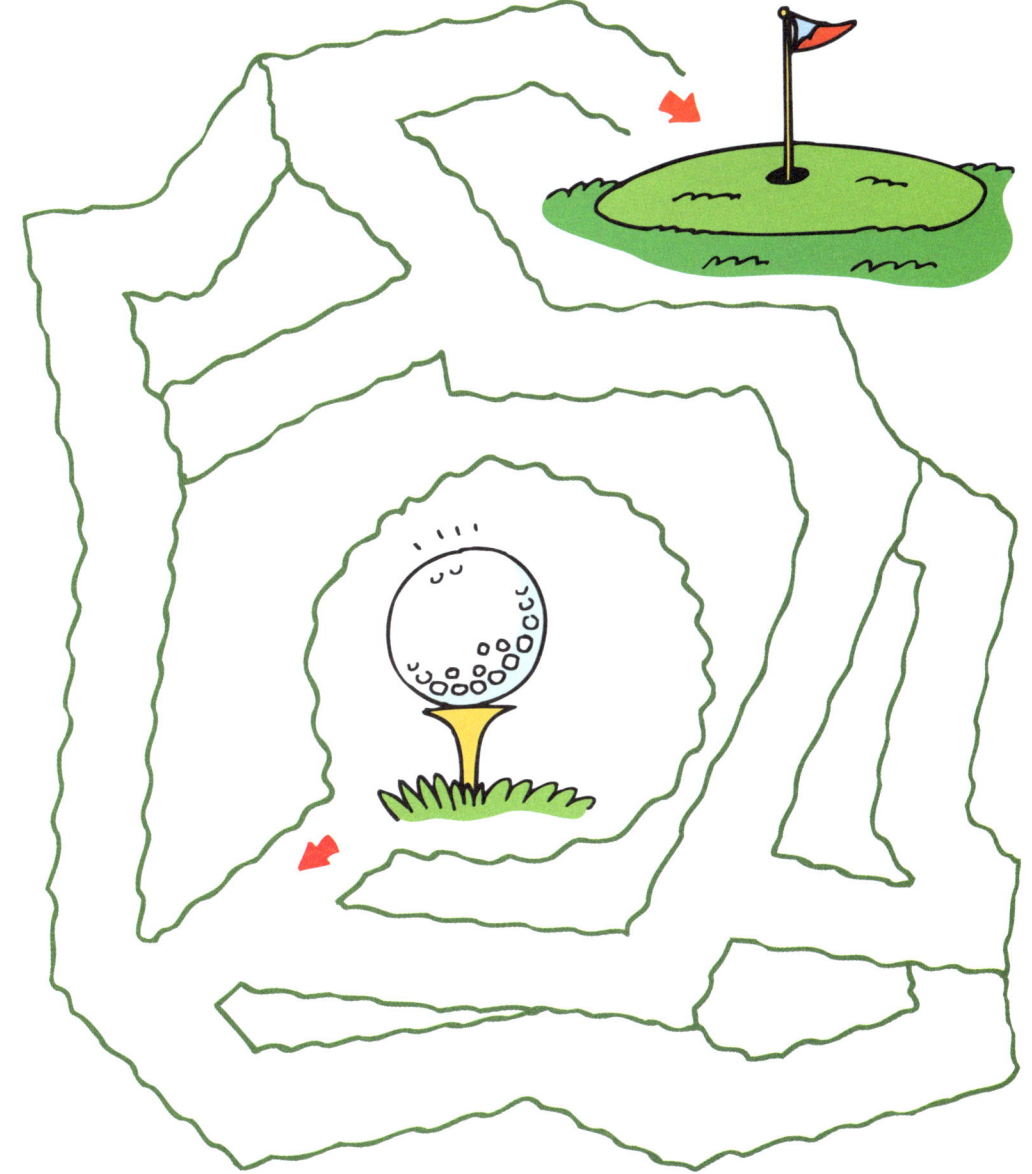

# Let's Swing

Color a path to the swing.

# Cookies

Color a path to the cookies.

# Happy Birthday

Help the bunny find her gifts.

# Time to Eat

Lead the pig to the corn.

# The Bookworm

Color a path through the book.

# To the City

Color a road to the city.

# Apple Snack

Color a path to the apple.

# Lost and Found

Find the lost puppy.

# Over the Net

Get the ball over the net.

# A Dancing Mouse

Color a path to the shoes.

# Score!

Color a path to the goal.

# Hungry Horse

Lead the horse to the carrot.

# Dirty Dishes

Help clean the dishes.

# Sleepy Dog

Color a path to the bed.

# On Sale

Color the ▢s to the sale.

# Baby's Bedtime

Color a path from **1** to **10** to the baby's bed.